This book belongs to:

_____

A

is for **Aretha Franklin**.
Betta R-E-S-P-E-C-T
this Queen of Soul.

B

is for **Bob Marley**, **Biz Markie** and **Beyonce**.
One Love for beatboxing and all hail to the soultress Queen "B."

D is for Diddy.

OR should we say Puff Daddy?
A dandy, dapper, and daring entrepreneur

E is for Earth, Wind & Fire.

Everyone, *Let's Groove* **Tonight!**

H is for Herbie Hancock.

**A Hyde Park Alum,
best Jazz artists to have ever come!**

I is for Ice Cube.

J is for **Jay Z** aka **Jiggaman**, one of the best rappers turned businessman out of Brooklyn.

K is for Kanye West.

Chicago's best, a musical genius!

L is for **Lauryn Hill.**

Lovely lyrics that my sistas can feel!

M

is for **Miles Davis**, *My Kind of Blue*,
a jazz composer, that trumpet he blew!
Gotta add **Michael Jackson**
or Moonwalker Mike - The King of Pop
that everyone across the world liked!
Oh what the heck,
let's add **Mariah Carey**
and **Mary J. Blige**,
this would be a magnificent quartet!

N is for New Edition.

A R&B group we could never forget!
Let's give it up for
Mike, Ronnie, Johnny,
Ralph, Bobby, and Rick!

O is for Outkast.

What an extraordinary rap sound, opened the doors for the whole A-town!

Q

is for **Quincy Jones**.
80 Grammy nominations
and 27 Grammy awards.
Q is a musical legend,
salute to our Chicago bredrin.

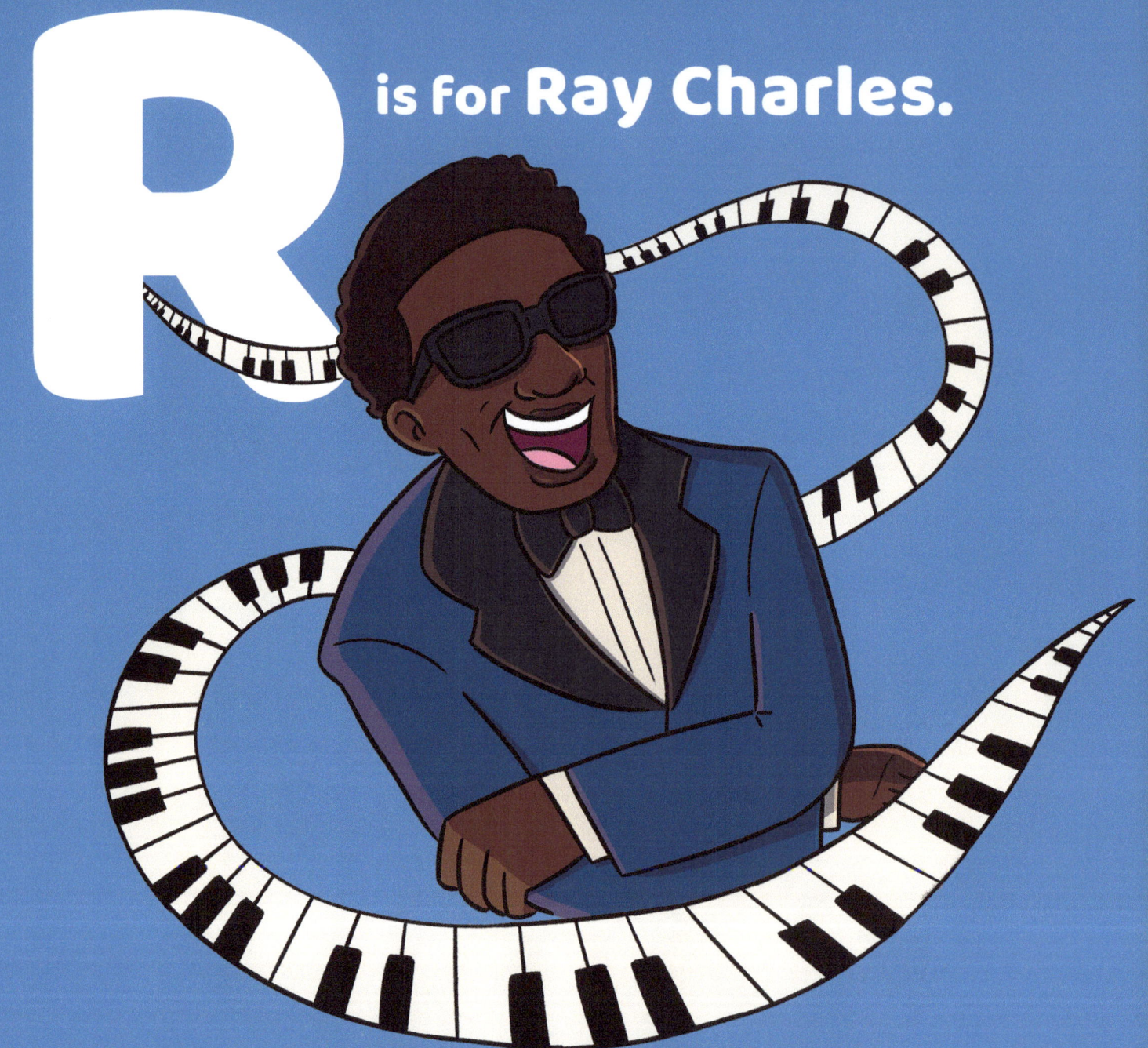

T is for The Temptations or TLC.

One Male, One Female group. Both share a similar tune, titled *Ain't 2 Proud 2 Beg*.

U is for Usher,

who is super unique. At the young age of six he was singing and dancing to the beat!

V is for Luther Vandross.

The only exception.
Because he's an outstanding vocalist
a *Superstar* we will remember *Always and Forever.*

Y is for **Yolanda Adams.**

The Queen of Gospel Music.

So many African American Musicians who have paved the way, thankful for all even if we didn't say. Please forgive me or should I say we.

Written by Lawson, Londyn, Dad, and Brittany.
This was African American Musicians ABC.
Peace out until next time!
Love, The Thomas Family.

www.ingramcontent.com/pod-product-compliance
Lightning Source LLC
Chambersburg PA
CBHW041154290426
44108CB00002B/64